The Voice of the Century

Collected by

Bob Hoffman

Copyright © 2009 by Bob Hoffman
All rights reserved

Hoffman, Bob
The Very Best Jokes of the Century/Bob Hoffman

ISBN: 978-1-61584-553-8

Without limiting the rights under copyright reserved above, no part of this publication may be reproduced, stored in or introduced into a retrieval system or transmitted in any form or by any means (electronic, mechanical, photocopying, recording or otherwise), without prior written permission of the copyright holder of this book.

Published in the United States of America

Edited by Maine Desk LLC
www.mainedesk.com

Printed by Morris Publishing
3212 East Highway 30
Kearney, NE 68847
800-650-7888

DEDICATION AND ACKNOWLEDGMENTS

This book is dedicated to two very special people who in their own way brought sunshine and fun into the lives of their many friends and especially in my own.

WILBUR TALISMAN

Twenty five years ago Wilbur began telling me jokes.
They were so good that I decided to save them.
And so began the start of a collection that became
The Very Best Jokes of The Century
Thanks a million for your help, Wilbur.

BOBBIE ROSEN

Bobbie was one of my best friends.
She left us many years ago, all too soon.
I will always remember the way she would
laugh uncontrollably when I told her one of my jokes.
Bobbie, now many other people will be able
to laugh at the jokes that you enjoyed.

Special Thanks

Special thanks to my long-suffering wife Evie who
has listened to my jokes over and over again and
never failed to laugh and enjoy them.

Many Thanks

Many thanks to my good friend Ernie Weiss,
an author in his own right,
whose encouragement, help, and advice
has aided me in the publication of this book.

Table of Contents

DEDICATION AND ACKNOWLEDGMENTS 3
JEWISH FIRE DEPARTMENT 11
CONFESSION 12
THE SECOND BALCONY 13
THE SECRET STORY OF HOW THE JEWS GOT THE TEN COMMANDMENTS 14
89-YEAR-OLD MAN 15
POLITE DINNER 16
A GREAT LOVER 17
ORGANIC VEGETABLES 18
A LAWYER WITH A HEART 19
PARROT 20
PUNS 21
A LONG TIME AGO 23
A 12-INCH PIANIST 25
A BRIDGE STORY 26
ON A CLEAR DAY 27
PENGUINS 29
A MAN IN GOOD HEALTH 30
PACKERS FAN 31
BLOOMINGDALE'S 32
THE WEDDING ANNIVERSARY 33
JEALOUS HUSBAND 35
CANNIBALS 36
RAINING 37
QUASIMODO 38

WHY PARENTS GO GREY	39
LAWYERS	41
COLD WEATHER	43
SPACE PEOPLE	44
HOTEL SOAP	45
THE FACELIFT	49
A NEW CAR	51
APPLYING FOR MEMBERSHIP IN THE BAPTIST CHURCH	52
EARS	53
HOME DEPOT SCAM	54
FREQUENTLY ASKED QUESTIONS ABOUT HEALTH CARE	55
CHILDREN	57
BEARS WARNING	58
THE MAN WITH BULGING EYES	59
THE FIRST JEWISH PRESIDENT	61
DIARY ENTRIES OF A YOUNG WOMAN ON A CRUISE SHIP	62
THE LOAN	63
MIRACLE	65
COW FROM MINSK	66
STRUDEL	67
DONALD DUCK AND MINNIE MOUSE	68
WAILING WALL	69
ICE FISHING	70
THE CAR	71
GRAPES	72
ELEMENTARY MY DEAR WATSON	73
THE INTERVIEW	74
THREE-LEGGED CHICKEN	75
ADAM'S RIB	76

NAVAL OPERATIONS	77
SINGLE LIFE	78
WORDS OF WISDOM	79
CIRCLES, SQUARES, AND TRIANGLES	81
THE MEMORIAL	82
RECIPE FOR BEST EVER CHOCOLATE RUM CAKE	83
SUPERMARKET CLERK	84
DOLLARS FOR ISRAEL	85
FRIENDLY WITCH	86
THE WATCH	87
VOW OF SILENCE	88
JOE'S BARBER SHOP	89
PROFESSIONAL RIVALRY	91
GOLF	92
THE GUEST	93
FOOD FOR THOUGHT	94
FATHER	95
HORSE RACING	96
THE SPOON	97
RODNEY DANGERFIELD'S BEST ONE-LINERS	99
A CHANCE ENCOUNTER	101
UNFAITHFUL WIFE	102
HOT DOGS	103
THE DONATION	104
FRIENDS	105
TWO PIECES OF STRING	106
TANDJEWBERRYMUD	107
WIDOWHOOD AND REMARRIAGE	109
NOTHING	110

ROOM 436	111
GOD	112
THE POPE	113
LIMERICKS	115
THE SHOPLIFTER	117
THE THIRSTY ARAB	118
THE GENIE	119
PIG	121
A PARKING SPACE	122
ARRANGED MARRIAGE	123
ABOUT THE AUTHOR	125

JEWISH FIRE DEPARTMENT

One dark night outside a small town near Poulsbo, Washington, a fire started inside the local chemical plant. In a blink of an eye it exploded into massive flames. The alarm went out to all fire departments for miles around.

When the volunteer firefighters appeared on the scene, the chemical company president rushed to the fire chief and said, "All our secret formulas are in the vault in the center of the plant. They must be saved! I will give $50,000 to the fire department that brings them out intact." But the roaring flames held the firefighters off.

Soon more fire departments had to be called in as the situation became desperate. As the firemen arrived, the president shouted out that the offer was now $100,000 to the fire department that could bring out the company's secret files.

From the distance, a lone siren was heard as another fire truck came into sight. It was the nearby Chasidic Jewish rural township volunteer fire company composed mainly of Jewish ultra-orthodox men over the age of 65. To everyone's amazement, that little run-down fire engine roared right past all the newer sleek engines that were parked outside the plant.

Without even slowing down it drove straight into the middle of the inferno. Outside, the other firemen watched as the Chasidic old timers jumped off right in the middle of the fire and fought it back on all sides. It was a performance and effort never seen before. Within a short time, the Chasidic old timers had extinguished the fire and had saved the secret formulas.

The grateful chemical company president announced that for such a superhuman feat he was upping the reward to $200,000 and walked over to personally thank each of the brave firefighters. The local TV news reporter rushed in to capture the event on film, asking their chief, "What are you going to do with all that money?"

"Vell," said Moishe Goldberg, the 70-year-old fire chief, "Da first thing ve gonna do is fix da brakes on dat freakin truck!"

CONFESSION

A rabbi and a priest, having grown up in the same neighborhood, were very good friends. One day when the rabbi was visiting his friend at the church, the priest got an urgent telephone call from one of his parishioners asking the priest to visit right away. The priest said that he would be there very soon, but realized that he was due to sit in the confessional. The priest asked the rabbi if he would take the priest's place for about an hour.

The rabbi said he would be glad to help out, but what did he know about sitting in a confessional?

The priest assured him that it was very easy. He said, "Watch me do the first one so that you can get the hang of it."

A man entered the booth and said to the priest, "Father, I have sinned."

The priest said, "Yes, my son?"

The man replied, "Father, this week I committed adultery three times."

The priest said, "That's terrible. Go home and say ten Hail Marys and leave $5 in the box on the way out."

Then the priest came out of the confessional and said to the rabbi, "See how easy it is?"

The rabbi answered, "Okay, I think I've got the hang of it."

The priest left and the rabbi went into the confessional box. Another man came into the box, sat down and said, "Father, I have sinned."

The rabbi said "Yes, my son?"

The man replied, "Father, this week I committed adultery one time."

The rabbi replied, "Go out and do it two more times. We have a special on this week—three for $5."

THE SECOND BALCONY

A man lay sprawled across three entire seats in the posh theater. When the usher came by and noticed this, he whispered to the man, "Sorry, sir, but you're only allowed one seat."

The man groaned but didn't budge. The usher became impatient.

"Sir, if you don't get up from there, I'm going to have to call the manager."

Again, the man just groaned, which infuriated the usher who turned and marched briskly back up the aisle in search of his manager. In a few moments, both the usher and the manager returned and stood over the man.

Together the two of them tried repeatedly to move him, but with no success. Finally, they summoned the police.

The cop surveyed the situation briefly then asked, "All right buddy, what's your name?"

"Sam," the man moaned.

"Where ya from, Sam?"

With pain in his voice Sam replied, "The second balcony."

THE SECRET STORY OF HOW THE JEWS GOT THE TEN COMMANDMENTS

One day God asked Moses to visit him on Mount Sinai. Moses climbed up the mountain and sat down on a rock and said, "I am here God, as you commanded me."

God said, "Moses, I called you here to give you these two tablets with Commandments inscribed on them."

Moses picked up the two tablets and said, "What do you wish me to do with these tablets?" But God had a lot of other things to do and had already left so he could not answer him.

Moses started down the mountain wondering what he was going do with these Commandments. Part way down the mountain he ran into a Frenchman. Moses said to the Frenchman, "How would you like a nice commandment today?"

The Frenchman said, "What kind of commandments do you have?"

Moses replied, "Here's a good one. 'Thou shalt not covet thy neighbor's wife.'"

"No thanks," said the Frenchman as he walked off.

Half way down the mountain Moses ran into an Arab and said to him, "How would you like one of my commandments?"

The Arab said, "What's a Commandment?"

Moses said, "I will give you an example of one. 'Thou shalt not steal.'"

The Arab said, "No way! I don't want to have anything to do with your Commandments! Find someone else."

At the bottom of the mountain a Jewish shepherd was going by with his flock. Moses said to him, "How would you like some of my nice Commandments?"

The Jewish Shepherd said, "How much are they?"

Moses said, "Nothing, they're free."

"Okay," said the Jewish shepherd. "I'll take ten."

89-YEAR-OLD MAN

An elderly man enters the confessional and says to the priest, "Father, I'm 89 years old, married, have four kids and eleven grandchildren, and last night I had an affair and made love to two 18-year-old-girls. Both of them. Twice."

The priest says, "Well, my son, when was the last time you went to confession?"

"Never, Father. I'm Jewish," answers the man.

The priest asks, "So then, why are you telling me?"

The elderly man says, "I'm telling everyone."

POLITE DINNER

There are two polite people having dinner together. On the table there is a dish with one big piece of fish and one small piece of fish. They politely say to each other, "You may choose first." "No, you may choose first." And this goes on for a while.

Then the first person says: "Okay, I'll take first." And he takes the BIG piece of fish.

The second person says, "Why did you take the big piece? That's not polite!"

The first person says, "Which piece would you have taken?"

The second person replies, "Why, I would have taken the SMALL piece, of course."

The first person says, "Well, that's what you've got!"

A GREAT LOVER

Zelda, Florence, and Miriam, three widows, were sitting together outside their apartment complex in Florida.

Zelda says, "My Sammy was such a lover—like you never saw. When he ran his hands over my body I would shiver all over."

Florence says, "My Morris was such a kisser. When he would kiss me, my hair would stand up straight."

Miriam says, "When my Schenley…"

Zelda cuts her off, and says, "Schenley is a liquor."

Miriam says, "You knew my Schenley?!"

ORGANIC VEGETABLES

Two men were talking one day. "My wife asked me to buy ORGANIC vegetables from the market garden," said the first man.

"So were you able to find some?" the second man asked.

"Well when I got to the market, I asked the gardener, 'These vegetables are for my wife. Have they been sprayed with any poisonous chemicals?' The gardener said 'No, you'll have to do that yourself.'"

A LAWYER WITH A HEART

One afternoon a lawyer was riding in his limousine when he saw two men along the roadside eating grass. Disturbed, he ordered his driver to stop and he got out to investigate.

He asked one of the men, "Why are you eating grass?"

"We don't have any money for food," the poor man replied. "We have to eat grass."

"Well then, you can come with me to my house and I'll feed you," the lawyer said.

"But sir, I have a wife and two children with me. They are over there, under that tree."

"Bring them along," the lawyer replied.

Turning to the other poor man, the lawyer said, "You come with us also."

In a pitiful voice, the second man replied, "But sir, I also have a wife and SIX children with me!"

"Bring them all!" the lawyer answered. They all entered the car, which was no easy task, even for a car as large as the limousine.

Once underway, one of the poor fellows turned to the lawyer and said, "Sir, you are too kind. Thank you for taking all of us with you."

The lawyer replied, "Glad to do it. You'll really love my place—the grass is almost a foot high."

PARROT

A magician is working on a small cruise ship. He's been doing his routines for two years now. The audiences appreciate him and they change often enough that he doesn't have to worry too much about new tricks. However there is a parrot that sits on a perch in the corner and watches him night after night.

Eventually, the parrot figures out how all the tricks work and starts giving it away for the audience. For example, when the magician makes a bouquet of flowers disappear, the parrot squawks, "Behind his back! It's behind his back!" The magician is really annoyed but doesn't know what to do since the parrot belongs to the captain of the ship.

One day while the magician is giving an exhibition and the parrot is giving away all his secrets, the ship's boiler explodes. Pieces of the ship are sent in all directions. The magician lands in the middle of the ocean safely. He swims to a large piece of wood that was part of the ship. He climbs onto the piece of wood and notices that the parrot is sitting there. The parrot keeps looking around at the ocean for about an hour and then says "Okay, I give up. Where did you hide the ship?"

PUNS

Two Eskimos sitting in a kayak were chilly, but when they lit a fire in the craft it sank—proving once and for all that you can't have your kayak and heat it, too.

~~~

Two boll weevils grew up in South Carolina. One went to Hollywood and became a famous actor. The other stayed behind in the cotton fields and never amounted to much. The second one, naturally, became known as, "The lesser of two weevils."

~~~

A mushroom walks into a bar, sits down and orders a drink. The bartender says, "We don't serve mushrooms here." The mushroom says, "Why not? I'm a fun guy!"

~~~

A guy goes into a restaurant for a Christmas breakfast while in his home town for the holidays. After looking over the menu he says, "I'll just have the eggs benedict." His order comes a while later and it's served on a huge fancy chrome plate. He asks the waiter, "What's with the fancy plate?"

The waiter replies, "There's no plate like chrome for the hollandaise!"

~~~

Very early one morning two birds are sitting at the side of a large puddle of oil. They see a worm on the other side. So, one flies over and the other one swims through. Which one gets to the worm first? The one who swam, of course, because, "Da oily boid gets da woim."

~~~

A neutron goes into a bar and asks the bartender, "How much for a beer?"

The bartender replies, "For you, no charge."

~~~

Two molecules are walking down the street and they run in to each other. One says to the other, "Are you all right?"

"No, I lost an electron!"

"Are you sure?"

"I'm positive!"

~~~

Did you hear about the Buddhist who refused his dentist's Novocaine during root canal work? He wanted to transcend dental medication.

A LONG TIME AGO

About a century or two ago, the Pope decided that all the Jews had to leave Rome. Naturally there was a big uproar from the Jewish community. So the Pope made a deal.

He would have a religious debate with a member of the Jewish community. If the Jew won, the Jews could stay. If the Pope won, the Jews would leave.

The Jews realized that they had no choice. So they picked a middle-aged man named Moishe to represent them.

Moishe asked for one condition in the debate. To make it more interesting, neither side would be allowed to talk.

The Pope agreed. The day of the great debate came. Moishe and the Pope sat opposite each other for a full minute before the Pope raised his hand and showed three fingers.

Moishe looked back at him and raised one finger.

The Pope waved his fingers in a circle around his head.

Moishe pointed to the ground where he sat.

The Pope pulled out a wafer and a glass of wine.

Moishe pulled out an apple.

The Pope stood up and said, "I give up. This man is too good. The Jews can stay."

An hour later, the cardinals were hovering around the Pope asking him what had happened. The Pope said, "First I held up three fingers to represent the Trinity. He responded by holding up one finger to remind me that there was still one God common to both our religions. Then I waved my finger around to show him that God was all around us. He responded by pointing to the ground and showing that God was also right here with us. I pulled out the wine and wafer to show that God absolves us from our sins. He pulled out an apple to remind me of the original sin. He had an answer for everything. What could I do?"

Meanwhile, the Jewish community had crowded around Moishe. "What happened?" they asked.

"Well," said Moishe, "First he said to me that the Jews had three days to get out of here. I told him that not one of us was leaving. Then he told me that this whole city would be cleared of Jews. I let him know that we were staying right here."

"Yes, yes…and then what?" asked the crowd.

"I don't know," said Moishe. "He took out his lunch, and I took out mine."

A 12-INCH PIANIST

A patron is sitting at a bar, and after a few drinks he takes a tiny piano and a little man about a foot tall out of his suitcase. The little man sits down at the piano and starts playing beautifully.

A fellow sitting next to the patron at the bar watches in sheer amazement. "That's unbelievable! Where on earth did you get him?"

"Well, I have this magic lamp here that was given to me by a genie."

"Could I try it?" asks the fellow.

"Sure, be my guest."

The fellow rubs the lamp, and out comes a handsome genie. "What do you wish?" asks the genie.

"I'd like a million bucks," says the fellow. Suddenly the room is filled with a million quacking ducks. The genie disappears back into the lamp.

"I asked for a million BUCKS, not a million DUCKS," the fellow says to the patron.

"I know," said the patron. "The genie is a little hard of hearing. You don't really think I asked for a 12-inch pianist, do you?"

A BRIDGE STORY

A housemaid was applying for a new position. When asked why she had left her last employment, she replied, "Well, sir, they paid good wages, but it was the strangest place I ever worked for. They played a card game called BRIDGE. And last night a lot of folks were there. As I was about to bring in the refreshments, I heard a man say, 'Lay down and let's see what you got.'

"Then another man said to a lady, 'Take your hand off my trick,'" and I pretty near dropped dead.

"And the lady answered, 'You forced me, you jumped me twice, when you didn't have the strength for another raise.'

"Another lady was talking and saying, 'Now it's time for me to play with your husband and you can play with mine.'

"Well, sir, just as I got my hat and coat and I was leaving, cross my heart and hope to die if one of them didn't say, 'Guess we'll go home soon, THIS IS MY LAST RUBBER!'"

ON A CLEAR DAY

One morning Warren woke up earlier than usual and feeling refreshed from a good night's sleep. He got up and started to prepare himself for the day's activities. He went outside and noticed that there wasn't a single cloud in the sky and that the temperature was in the seventies. He decided that this would be a perfect day to enjoy his favorite hobby, namely, mountain climbing. He called up all of his friends and asked each one to join him for a hike, but everyone offered some sort of excuse that prevented them from joining him. Even so, he was so caught up in the beautiful day that he decided that he would climb a mountain by himself.

He gathered up his ropes, backpack, climbing shoes, and other paraphernalia that he needed for his hike. He headed off by himself to a nearby mountain. When he finally arrived at the mountain he planned his ascent. The mountain was quite high and would be a challenge to any climber. However, Warren was an experienced climber and overcoming all obstacles made his way to the very top. Exhausted, Warren lay down on the ground and took a short catnap.

When he woke up he arose and looked around. He went to the edge of the mountain and looked out over the countryside. He could see for miles and miles in all directions. "What a wonderful sight on such a perfect day!" he thought.

Suddenly, without warning some of the ground at the edge of the cliff began to come loose. Warren slipped on the loose stones and lost his balance, plummeting over the cliff and hurtling downward. Halfway down a branch hung out from the mountain and Warren was able to catch the branch and break his fall. He looked in all directions. Downward about 2000 feet and upwards 3000 feet and in front of him was a sheer wall with no possible footholds. Holding on for dear life he looked up and called out. "Is anyone up there?"

"I'm up here," came a strange voice.

"Who are you?" asked Warren.

"I'm God," said the voice.

"Thank goodness!" said Warren. "Can you get me out of this predicament?"

"Yes, I can help you but first I must ask you some questions and put you to a test. Do you agree to my conditions?"

"Yes, yes I agree anything at all," said Warren. "Please help me!"

"Very well. Do you believe in me?"

"Absolutely, I go to church every Sunday morning," answered Warren.

"Very well, listen carefully to what I say. Now comes the test of your faith in me. I want you to let go of the branch with your left hand."

"Alright," said Warren, "I've let go of the branch with my left hand."

"Now," said God, "I want you to let go of the branch with your right hand."

There is silence for thirty seconds and then Warren said, "Is there anyone else up there?"

PENGUINS

There is a guy who is driving like a bat out of hell down Atlantic Avenue. A policeman spots him and blows his whistle, pulling him off the road. The policeman walks over to the car and says, "Hey fella, do you realize that you were going 50 miles an hour in a 30 mile an hour zone? You're going to get a ticket for speeding."

"I'm sorry officer," says the driver, "I'm just very upset."

The officer looks in the backseat of the car and sees three penguins sitting there. He says, "What's with the penguins?"

The driver says, "Oh, that's what I'm upset about. You see my best friend just died and left these penguins to me in his will and I don't know what to do with them."

"Well," says the officer, "Why don't you take them to the zoo?"

"Hey that's a great idea!" says the driver and after receiving the ticket takes off in the direction of Marblehead.

The next day the same driver is going like a bat out of hell down Humphrey Street and the same officer spots him and pulls him over to the side of the road. The officer walks over to the car and says, "Okay fella, what's the big...oh, it's you again."

"I'm awfully sorry officer," says the driver, "I didn't realize how fast I was going."

The officer looks in the back seat and sees the three penguins sitting there, each wearing a pair of sunglasses. He says, "What's with these penguins? I thought you were going to take them to the zoo?"

The driver answers, "Oh, that was yesterday. Today we're going to the beach."

A MAN IN GOOD HEALTH

Morris Schwartz went for his annual checkup to his internist Dr. Throckman. Dr. Throckman ran a series of tests on Morris and then asked him to come to his office.

The doctor says, "Mr. Schwartz, you are in superb condition for a man of 85 years."

"I know," Morris answers. "God looks after me."

"How so?" asks Dr. Throckman.

"Well," says Morris, "God knows that I don't see well. So when I wake up in the middle of the night and go into the bathroom, God turns the light on when I enter and turns the light off when I leave."

Dr. Throckman is concerned about what Morris has told him. So he decides to call up Morris's wife and tell her what Morris has said about God looking out for him.

"Mrs. Schwartz, first I want to tell you that your husband had a great checkup and is in very good health. However, I am concerned when he claims that God looks after him. He says that when he goes into the bathroom at night God turns on the light, and when he leaves the bathroom God turns the light off."

"Oh no!" says Mrs. Schwartz. "Don't tell me he's peeing in the refrigerator again!"

PACKERS FAN

There was a Packers fan with a really crappy seat at Lambeau Stadium. Looking through his binoculars, he spotted an empty seat on the 50-yard line. Thinking to himself, "What a waste," he made his way down to the empty seat.

When he arrived at the seat, he asked the man sitting next to it, "Is this seat taken?"

The man replied, "This was my wife's seat. She passed away. She was a big Packers fan."

The other man replied, "I'm so sorry to hear of your loss. May I ask why you didn't give the ticket to a friend or a relative?"

The man replied, "They're all at the funeral."

BLOOMINGDALE'S

A blind man, with a seeing eye dog, walks into Bloomingdale's Department Store. He goes to the middle of the store, picks up the dog by the tail and starts whirling him around over his head.

The manager, greatly concerned, runs over to the blind man and says, "What are you doing?"

The blind man says, "Oh, just looking around."

THE WEDDING ANNIVERSARY

Milton and Ethel have been married 50 years. Their children decide to host a big party for them at the Hilton Hotel. Three hundred people are invited and everyone has a good time.

When the party is over, Milton and Ethel retire to the wedding suite of the hotel, which they have taken for the weekend. They are preparing for bed and Milton says, "You know what Ethel?"

She says, "What Milton?"

He says, "I think that was the best party I ever went to."

She says, " I think you're right, it was a wonderful time."

He says, "Ethel, I want to thank you for 50 wonderful years."

"And I want to thank you also Milton."

"Ethel, I would like to ask you a very personal question and I hope you will answer honestly."

"Oh, I certainly will Milton, I certainly will. Ask me anything."

"Ethel, in the 50 years that we have been happily married have you ever been unfaithful to me?"

She says, "Only three times Milton."

"Oh my God, when was the first time?"

"Do you remember, Milton, when you went to the bank to borrow $250,000 so you could go into business for yourself and they turned you down? Well, that night I slept with the president of the bank. And remember the next day they called you up and gave you the loan?"

"Oh, Ethel, I owe my business career to you, thank you. Okay, now when was the second time?"

"Milton, do you remember when you had your heart attack and you needed open heart surgery and you called up Dr. Debakey, but he was too busy to work you in? And two days later, he called up and said he would be happy to operate?"

"Oh Ethel, I owe my life to you. Alright now, what about the third time?"

"Milton, do you remember when you were running for President of the Synagogue and you were 35 votes short?"

JEALOUS HUSBAND

A man calls his home. The maid answers the phone and he asks to speak to his wife. The maid says, "Um, uh, well, uh…"

He says, "I said, let me talk to my wife."

She says, "Well she's not downstairs."

He says, "Where is she?"

She says, "She's upstairs."

"What is she doing upstairs?" he asks.

The maid answers, "Well, um, uh I think she's in the bedroom with the gardener."

The man says, "Oh my God this is terrible! Here's what I want you to do. I want you to take the sharpest carving knife from the kitchen and go upstairs and stab them both to death. I'll hold the line."

The maid says, "Okay." Ten minutes later the maid returns and says, "Sir!"

"Yes?" he says.

"It's done."

"Good. Now here's what I want to do. Drag the bodies down the stairs into the backyard and throw them into the swimming pool."

The maid says, "Sir…"

He says, "Yes?"

"We don't have a swimming pool!"

"IS THIS 745-8743?"

CANNIBALS

A sailor is stranded on a desert island. He thought the island was deserted, but he was captured by a tribe of cannibals. The cannibals are about to kill the sailor but the sailor protests claiming that he is a "great warrior."

The Chief of the tribe steps in and says, "If you can prove that you are a great warrior we will not kill you!" The Chief thinks to himself and then says, "To prove you are a great warrior you must pass three tests. If you pass these tests, we will let you live." The sailor says, "All right, I accept the challenge. What are the three tests?"

The Chief explains, "There are three tents. In the first tent is a jug of wine You must drink this jug of wine in ten minutes and not get sick. In the second tent is a tiger with an impacted wisdom tooth. You must extract the tooth from the tiger. In the third tent is my DAUGHTER!! She has already killed two husbands who could not satisfy her. You must enter her tent and satisfy her!"

The sailor begins the tests. He enters the first tent and nine minutes later he walks out staggering and swinging the empty jug of wine. He doesn't get sick, so he passes the first test. He then enters the second tent and there are horrible sounds from the tiger who is screeching, screaming, and growling. After about 20 minutes the sailor comes out of the tent, with scratches, cuts, torn clothes and says, "Okay, now where's that lady with the toothache?!"

RAINING

A woman is in bed with her boyfriend when she hears her husband's car pull into the driveway. "Hurry!" she yells to him. "Grab your clothes and jump out of the window!"

The boyfriend looks out the window and replies, "I can't jump out there—it's raining!"

"Jump or he'll kill us both!" shouts the woman. So the boyfriend jumps out the window. As he sprints down the street, he discovers he's run right into the middle of a town marathon. He starts running alongside the others and, though he is naked, tries to blend in as best he can. One of the runners asks him, "Do you always run in the nude?"

The boyfriend replies, "Oh, yes, it feels so good with the air blowing over your skin."

"And do you always wear a condom?"

The boyfriend replies, "Only when it's raining!"

QUASIMODO

After Quasimodo's death, the bishop of the Cathedral of Notre Dame sent word through the streets of Paris that a new bell ringer was needed. The bishop decided that he would conduct the interviews personally and went up into the belfry to begin the screening process. After observing several applicants demonstrate their skills, he had decided to call it a day when an armless man approached him and announced that he was there to apply for the bell ringer's job. The bishop was incredulous. "You have no arms!"

No matter," said the man. "Observe!" And he began striking the bells with his face, producing a beautiful melody on the carillon. The bishop listened in astonishment, convinced that he finally found a suitable replacement for Quasimodo. But suddenly, rushing forward to strike a bell, the armless man tripped and plunged headlong out of the belfry window to his death in the street below.

The stunned bishop rushed to his side. When he reached the street, a crowd had gathered around the fallen figure, drawn by the beautiful music they had heard only moments before. As they silently parted to let the bishop through, one of them asked, "Bishop, who was this man?"

"I don't know his name," the bishop sadly replied, "but his face rings a bell."

The following day, despite the sadness that weighed heavily on his heart due to the unfortunate death of the armless campanologist, the bishop continued his interviews for the bell ringer of Notre Dame. The first man to approach him said, "Your Excellency, I am the brother of the poor armless wretch who fell to his death from this very belfry yesterday. I pray that you honor his life by allowing me to replace him in this duty."

The bishop agreed to give the man an audition, and as the armless man's brother stooped to pick up a mallet to strike the first bell, he groaned, clutched at his chest and died on the spot.

Two monks, hearing the bishop's cries of grief at this second tragedy, rushed up the stairs to his side. "What has happened? Who is this man?" the first monk asked breathlessly.

"I don't know his name," sighed the distraught bishop, "but he's a dead ringer for his brother."

WHY PARENTS GO GREY

The boss of a big company needed to call one of his employees about an urgent problem with one of the main computers. He dialed the employee's home phone number and was greeted with a child's whispered, "Hello?"

Feeling put out at the inconvenience of having to talk to a youngster, the boss asked, "Is your Daddy home?"

"Yes," whispered the small voice.

"May I talk with him?" the man asked.

To the surprise of the boss, the small voice whispered, "No."

Wanting to talk with an adult, the boss asked, "Is your Mommy there?"

"Yes," came the answer.

"May I talk with her?"

Again the small voice whispered, "No."

Knowing that it was unlikely that a young child would be left home alone, the boss decided he would just leave a message with the person who should be there watching over the child. "Is there any one there besides you?" the boss asked the child.

"Yes" whispered the child, "A policeman."

Wondering what a cop would be doing at his employee's home, the boss asked, "May I speak with the policeman"?

"No, he's busy," whispered the child.

"Busy doing what?" asked the boss.

"Talking to Daddy and Mommy and the Fireman," came the whispered answer.

Growing concerned and even worried as he heard what sounded like a helicopter through the ear piece on the phone the boss asked, "What is that noise?"

"A hello-copper," answered the whispering voice.

"What is going on there?" asked the boss, now alarmed.

In an awed, whispering voice the child answered, "The search team just landed the hello-copper."

Alarmed, concerned, and more than just a little frustrated the boss asked, "Why are they there?"

Still whispering, the young voice replied, "They're looking for me."

LAWYERS

A recent edition of the Massachusetts Bar Association Lawyers Journal noted the following questions that actually were asked of witnesses by attorneys during trials, and, in certain cases, the responses given by insightful witnesses.

Q: "Is your appearance here this morning pursuant to a deposition notice which I sent to your attorney?

A: "No, this is how I dress when I go to work."

~~~

Q: "Doctor, how many autopsies have you performed on dead people?"

A: "All my autopsies are performed on dead people."

~~~

Q: "All your responses must be oral, okay? What school did you go to?"

A: "Oral."

~~~

Q: "Do you recall the time that you examined the body?"

A: "The autopsy started around 8:30 p.m."

Q: "And Mr. Dennington was dead at the time?"

A: "No, he was sitting on the table wondering why I was doing an autopsy."

~~~

Q: "Are you qualified to give a urine sample?"

A: "I have been since early childhood."

~~~

Q: "Doctor, before you performed the autopsy, did you check for a pulse?"

A: "No."

Q: "Did you check for breathing?"

A: "No."

Q: "So, then it is possible that the patient was alive when you began the autopsy?"

A: "No."

Q: "How can you be so sure, Doctor?"

A: "Because his brain was sitting in a jar on my desk."

Q: "But could the patient have still been alive nevertheless?"

A: "It is possible that he could have been alive and practicing law somewhere."

COLD WEATHER

It was autumn, and the Indians on the remote reservation asked their new Chief if the winter was going to be cold or mild. Since he was an Indian Chief in a modern society, he had never been taught the old secrets, and when he looked at the sky, he couldn't tell what the weather was going to be. Nevertheless, to be on the safe side, he replied to his tribe that the winter was indeed going to be cold and that the members of the village should collect wood to be prepared. But also being a practical leader, after several days he got an idea. He went to the phone booth, called the National Weather Service and asked, "Is the coming winter going to be cold?"

"It looks like this winter is going to be quite cold indeed," the meteorologist at the weather service responded.

So the Chief went back to his people and told them to collect even more wood in order to be prepared. A week later he called the National Weather Service again. "Is it going to be a very cold winter?"

"Yes," the man at National Weather Service again replied, "it's going to be a very cold winter."

The Chief again went back to his people and ordered them to collect every scrap of wood they could find. Two weeks later he called the National Weather Service again. "Are you absolutely sure that the winter is going to be very cold?"

"Absolutely," the man replied. "It's going to be one of the coldest winters ever."

"How can you be so sure?" the Chief asked.

The weatherman replied, "The Indians are collecting wood like crazy."

SPACE PEOPLE

A couple from Mars lands on the earth and soon meet up with an Earth couple. They hit it off well and begin asking questions and learning about life on each other's planets. Eventually, the conversation turns to the question of sex. Each couple tries to explain how they mate, but they find it somewhat difficult to explain. Neither can understand what is being described so one of the ladies suggests they switch partners for an evening so they can get a better understanding.

The Earth woman and Mars man go into the bedroom and they undress. The Earth woman says, "Gee, you're small!"

The Mars man says, "No problem," and hits his forehead and it grows longer.

The Earth woman is amazed and says, "Not bad."

The Mars man hits his forehead again and it grows even longer. The Earth woman is pleased but says, "It's kind of narrow."

The Mars man pulls on his ears and gets thicker. The Earth woman says, "Not bad." The Earth woman is finally pleased, so they get busy with the act.

The following morning the two couples meet in the lobby and the Earth man asks his wife how it went. She says, "It's the best I've ever had. How about you?"

The Earth man says, "I have such a headache. All night long she kept hitting me on the forehead and pulling my ears."

HOTEL SOAP

The following letters are taken from an actual incident between a London hotel and one of its guests. The hotel ended up submitting the letters to the London *Sunday Times*.

Dear Maid,

Please do not leave any more of those little bars of soap in my bathroom since I have brought my own bath-sized Dial. Please remove the six unopened little bars from the shelf under the medicine chest and another three in the shower soap dish. They are in my way.

Thank you, S. Berman

Dear Room 635,

I am not your regular maid. She will be back tomorrow, Thursday, from her day off. I took the three hotel soaps out of the shower soap dish as you requested. The six bars on your shelf I took out of your way and put on top of your Kleenex dispenser in case you should change your mind. This leaves only the three bars I left today per my instructions from the management to leave three soaps daily. I hope this is satisfactory.

Kathy, Relief Maid

Dear Maid,

I hope you are my regular maid. Apparently Kathy did not tell you about my note to her concerning little bars of soap. When I got back to my room this evening I found you had added three little bars of Camay to the shelf under my medicine cabinet. I am going to be here in the hotel for 2 weeks and have brought my own bath-size Dial so I won't need those six little bars on the shelf. They are in my way when shaving, brushing teeth, etc. Please remove them.

S. Berman

Dear Mr. Berman,

My day off was last Wednesday, so the relief maid left three hotel soaps as we are instructed to do by the management. I took the six soaps that were in your way on the shelf and put them in the soap dish where your Dial was. I put the Dial in the medicine cabinet for your convenience. I didn't remove the three complimentary soaps which are always placed inside the medicine cabinet for all new check-ins and which you did not object to when you checked in last Monday. Please let me know if I can be of further assistance.

Your regular maid, Dotty

Dear Mr. Berman,

The assistant manager, Mr. Kensedder, informed me this morning that you called him last evening and said you were unhappy with your maid service. I have assigned a new girl to your room. I hope you will accept my apologies for any past inconvenience. If you have any future complaints please contact me so I can give it my personal attention. Call extension 1108 between 8 am and 5 pm.

Thank you.

Elaine Carmen, Housekeeper

Dear Miss Carmen,

It is impossible to contact you by phone since I leave the hotel for business at 7:45 am and don't get back before 5:30 or 6 pm. That's the reason I called Mr. Kensedder last night. You were already off duty. I only asked Mr. Kensedder if he could do anything about those little bars of soap. The new maid you assigned me must have thought I was a new check-in today, since she left another three bars of hotel soap in my medicine cabinet along with her regular delivery of three bars on the bathroom shelf. In just 5 days here I have accumulated 24 little bars of soap. Why are you doing this to me?

S. Berman

Dear Mr. Berman,

Your maid, Kathy, has been instructed to stop delivering soap to your room and remove the extra soaps. If I can be of further assistance, please call extension 1108 between 8 am and 5 pm.

Thank you.

Elaine Carmen, Housekeeper

Dear Mr. Kensedder,

My bath-size Dial is missing. Every bar of soap was taken from my room including my own bath-size Dial. I came in late last night and had to call the bellhop to bring me four little bars of Cashmere Bouquet.

S. Berman

Dear Mr. Berman,

I have informed our housekeeper, Elaine Carmen, of your soap problem. I cannot understand why there was no soap in your room since our maids are instructed to leave three bars of soap each time they service a room. The situation will be rectified immediately. Please accept my apologies for the inconvenience.

Martin L. Kensedder, Assistant Manager

Dear Mrs. Carmen,

Who the hell left 54 little bars of Camay in my room? I came in last night and found 54 little bars of soap. I don't want 54 little bars of Camay. I want my one damn bar of bath-size Dial. Do you realize I have 54 bars of soap in here? All I want is my bath-size Dial. Please give me back my bath-size Dial.

S. Berman

Dear Mr. Berman,

You complained of too much soap in your room, so I had them removed. Then you complained to Mr. Kensedder that all your soap was missing, so I personally returned them—the 24 bars of Camay which had been taken, and the three bars of Camay you are supposed to receive daily. I don't know anything about the four bars of Cashmere Bouquet. Obviously your maid, Kathy, did not know I had returned your soaps, so she also brought 24 bars of Camay, plus the three daily bars of Camay.

I don't know where you got the idea this hotel issues bath-size Dial. I was able to locate some bath-size Ivory, which I left in your room.

Elaine Carmen, Housekeeper

Dear Mrs. Carmen,

Just a short note to bring you up-to-date on the latest soap inventory. As of today, there are on the shelf under medicine cabinet 18 bars of Camay in four stacks of four, and one stack of two. On the Kleenex dispenser there are 11 Camay in two stacks of four and one stack of three. On the bedroom dresser there are one stack of three Cashmere Bouquet, one stack of four hotel-size Ivory, and eight Camay in two stacks of four. Inside the medicine cabinet there are 14 Camay in three stacks of four and one stack of two. In the shower soap dish there are six Camay, very moist. On the northeast corner of the bathtub there is one bar of Cashmere Bouquet, slightly used. On the northwest corner of the bathtub there are six bars of Camay in two stacks of three.

Please ask Kathy when she services my room to make sure the stacks are neatly piled and dusted. Also, please advise her that stacks of more than four have a tendency to tip. May I suggest that my bedroom windowsill is not in use and will make an excellent spot for future soap deliveries?

One more item: I have purchased another bar of bath-sized Dial, which I am keeping in the hotel vault in order to avoid further misunderstandings.

Sincerely, S. Berman

THE FACELIFT

Sarah Goldstein, a widow, who had lost her husband 2 years before, was sitting in her living room contemplating the absence of excitement in her life.

It occurred to her that maybe she should spruce herself up and try to get a little more fun out of life. She looked in the mirror and noted that she had a lot of wrinkles and lines on her face. So, she decided that she would make an appointment with a surgeon to find out how much a facelift would cost.

She arrived at the doctor's office on the next Thursday and was given a thorough examination. The doctor assured her that she was a perfect candidate for a facelift and that the operation would be very successful.

Sarah was happy to hear the good news and asked the Doctor how much the operation would cost. He said, "The cost of the operation would be $20,000."

"Oh my, that's a lot of money, I will have to think about this." Sarah thought it over at home in her living room. She realized that $20,000 was a lot of money, and she would not want to spend that amount of money if she was not going to live a long time. She thought, "If only I could speak to God and find out how long I am going to live."

Just then she heard a voice that seemed to come from above. It said, "Sarah, this is God speaking. I have heard your wish and I am pleased to tell you to go ahead and have the operation."

Sarah was ecstatic over God's advice and arranged to have the operation. Two weeks after the facelift, Sarah looked in the mirror and was so pleased with the results that she decided to go shopping and buy herself a new outfit. While crossing the street to enter the Mall, she was struck by a bus and killed.

Sarah was furious as she approached the Pearly Gates. She said to Saint Peter, "I want to see the Boss. I have a bone to pick with him."

"I am sorry but the Boss is very busy and can't see you." Sarah carried on so much that Saint Peter finally agreed to try to get her an immediate appointment. He left for a moment, and when he came back he notified her that the Boss would see her now.

Sarah barged into God's office and said, "How could you do this to me? You told me I would live a long time and to have the operation, which cost me $20,000, and then you let me be run over by a bus?"

God looked at Sarah and said, "Was that you, Sarah? You looked so good, I didn't recognize you."

A NEW CAR

Vun day, Chaim vas walking down da street ven who did he see driving a brand new Chevrolet? It was Moishe!! Moishe pulled up to him mit a vide smile.

"Moishe, vere did you get dat car?" Chaim asked.

"Rochel gave it to me."

"She gave it to you? I knew she was sweet on you, but dis?"

"Vell let me tell you vot happened. Ve were driving out on country road 6, in the middle of novere. Rochel pulled off the road into da woods. She parked, got out of da car, trew off all her clothes and said "Moishe take vatever you vant.'… So I took da car."

"Moishe, you're a smart man, dem clothes never voulda fit ya."

APPLYING FOR MEMBERSHIP IN THE BAPTIST CHURCH

Three couples were applying for membership in the local Baptist Church. The minister explained to them that they would have to pass a simple test. In order to become members of the church, each of the three couples would have to abstain from sexual activity for a period of 4 weeks.

The three couples agreed to the terms, assuring the minister that there would be no problem. Four weeks later they all appeared before the minister for interrogation.

The minister asked the first couple if they had abstained from sex for the period of 4 weeks. They replied that they had had no problem complying with the terms of the application. The minister said that in that case they would be accepted into the congregation.

The minister then asked the second couple how they had made out during the past 4 weeks. They replied that they had trouble in the fourth week but the husband had moved into the spare bedroom and that solved the problem. The minister said that he was glad that the couple had been able to overcome their temptations and that the membership would be happy to welcome them into the church.

The minister then turned his attention to the third couple and said to them, "How did you make out with your attempt to abstain from sex during the previous 4 weeks?"

The husband spoke up and said, "Well, we were doing well for the first 3 weeks despite the temptations that were thrown in our way. A bad problem arose during the fourth week when my wife was trying to reach for a can of peas. The can fell from her grasp and landed on the floor. When she bent over to pick up the can of peas, I was no longer able to control myself and we had uncontrolled sex on the floor."

The minister said, "Well, that's too bad, but you understand the conditions that you had to live up to. I'm afraid that you will not be able to come into this church."

The wife said, "That's nothing. We also can't go back to the Supermarket any more."

EARS

A guy comes into work one day with both of his ears bandaged. One of his fellow workers looks at him and asks, "What happened to your ears?"

He says, "Yesterday I was ironing a shirt when the telephone rang and I accidentally answered the iron."

"Well, that explains one ear, but what happened to the other ear?"

He says, "Well, jeez, I had to call the doctor, didn't I?"

HOME DEPOT SCAM

This is a "heads up" for men who may be regular customers.

This one caught me by surprise. Over the last month I became a victim of a clever scam while out shopping. Simply going out to get supplies has turned out to be quite traumatic. Don't be naïve enough to think it couldn't happen to you or your friends.

Here's how the scam works. Two seriously good-looking 20-year-old girls come over to your car as you are packing your shopping into the trunk. They both start wiping your windshield with a rag and Windex, with their breasts almost falling out of their skimpy T-shirts. It is impossible not to look.

When you thank them and offer them a tip, they say "No," and instead ask you for a ride to McDonald's. You agree and they get in the back seat.

On the way they start undressing. Then one of them climbs over into the front seat and starts crawling all over you, while the other one steals your wallet.

I had my wallet stolen on May 4th, 9th, 10th, twice on the 15th, 17th, 20th, 24th, and 29th.

Also June 1st, 4th, twice on the 8th, 16th, 23rd, 26th, three times last Saturday, and very likely again this upcoming weekend.

So tell your friends to be careful.

FREQUENTLY ASKED QUESTIONS ABOUT HEALTH CARE

Q. I just joined a new HMO. How difficult will it be to choose the doctor I want?

A. Just slightly more difficult than choosing your parents. Your insurer will provide you with a book listing all the doctors who were participating in the plan at the time the information was gathered. These doctors basically fall into two categories: those who are no longer accepting new patients, and those who will see you but are no longer part of the plan. But don't worry; the remaining doctor who is still in the plan and accepting new patients has an office just a half-day's drive away!

Q. What does HMO stand for?

A. This is actually a variation of the phrase, "Hey, Moe!" Its roots go back to a concept pioneered by Doctor Moe Howard, who discovered that a patient could be made to forget about the pain in his foot if he was poked hard enough in the eye. Modern practice replaces the physical finger poke with high-tech equivalents such as voice mail and referral slips, but the result remains the same.

Q. Do all diagnostic procedures require pre-certification?

A. No. Only those you need.

Q. What are pre-existing conditions?

A. This is a phrase used by the grammatically challenged when they want to talk about existing conditions. Unfortunately, we appear to be pre-stuck with it.

Q. Well, can I get coverage for my pre-existing conditions?

A. Certainly, as long as they don't require any treatment.

Q. What happens if I want to try alternative forms of medicine?

A. You'll need to find alternative forms of payment.

Q. My pharmacy plan only covers generic drugs, but I need the name brand. I tried the generic medication, but it gave me a stomachache. What should I do?

A. Poke yourself in the eye.

Q. I have an 80/20 plan with a $200 deductible and a $2,000 yearly cap. My insurer reimbursed the doctor for my outpatient surgery, but I'd already paid my bill. What should I do?

A. You have two choices. Your doctor can sign the reimbursement check over to you, or you can ask him to invest the money for you in one of those great offers that only doctors and dentists hear about, like windmill farms or frog hatcheries.

Q. What should I do if I get sick while traveling?

A. Try sitting in a different part of the bus.

Q. No, I mean what if I'm away from home and I get sick?

A. You really shouldn't do that. You'll have a hard time seeing your primary care physician. It's best to wait until you return, and then get sick.

Q. I think I need to see a specialist, but my doctor insists he can handle my problem. Can a general practitioner really perform a heart transplant right in his office?

A. Hard to say, but considering that all you're risking is the $10 co-payment, there's no harm giving him a shot at it, eh?

Q. Will health care be any different in the next century?

A. No, but if you call right now, you might get an appointment by then.

CHILDREN

An elderly lady is sunning herself on a bench just outside the front entrance of the high-rise complex where she lives in Boca Raton, Florida.

The front door opens and out comes another elderly woman.

She walks very slowly over to the bench and sits down. She says, "Oy."

The first lady says, "I thought we agreed that we would not talk about the children."

BEARS WARNING

The Alaska Department of Fish and Game recently issued this bulletin:

"In light of the rising frequency of human/grizzly bear conflicts, the Alaska Department of Fish and Game is advising hikers, hunters, and fishermen to take extra precautions and keep alert for bears while in the field.

"We advise outdoorsmen to wear noisy little bells on their clothing so as not to startle unsuspecting bears. We also advise outdoorsmen to carry pepper spray in case of an encounter with a bear. It is also a good idea to watch out for fresh signs of bear activity.

"Outdoorsmen should recognize the difference between black bear and grizzly bear manure. Black bear manure is smaller and contains lots of berries and squirrel fur. Grizzly bear manure has little bells in it and smells like pepper."

THE MAN WITH BULGING EYES

Mort knew he was probably oversensitive about the problem, but the fact was that his eyes bulged. He went to doctor after doctor, but none seemed to know of any treatment.

In desperation, he looked up "Eye, Bulging" in the Yellow Pages. Sure enough a doctor was listed, and a few days later Mort found himself sitting on a vinyl couch in a seedy waiting room. A little nervous about being the only patient, he reminded himself how rare the condition was and that the doctor was a specialist.

At long last he was admitted to the doctor's office and examined. The doctor leaned back and informed him that there was a remedy, but not an easy one. "I must cut off your testicles," he said.

Mort's eyes bulged even more as he headed for the door. But after a few weeks of thinking it over, Mort acknowledged that his bulging eyes were what kept him from having sex in the first place, so he decided to go ahead with the operation.

He had the operation, and sure enough, his eyeballs sank back into their sockets most agreeably. In fact, he looked better than normal; he was actually handsome. Delighted, he thanked the doctor profusely, and decided to treat himself to a new suit.

"Charcoal gray pinstripe," he instructed the tailor. "Medium lapel, no cuffs."

"Fine," said the tailor, nodding. "Come back on Tuesday."

"Aren't you going to measure me?" asked Mort.

"Nah, I've been at this over 30 years, I can tell your size just by looking," the tailor assured him.

"That's impossible," blurted Mort.

"Size 42 jacket, right?"

"Yes," admitted Mort, amazed.

"Inseam 32 inches, right?" Mort nodded, dumbstruck.

"Thirty-six inch waist?" Again, Mort nodded.

"And you wear size 40 underwear, right?" concluded the tailor.

"Nope!" Mort told him. "Size 34."

"Listen, you can't fool me," said the tailor wearily. "Don't try to put one over on me."

"I'm telling you, I wear size 34 underwear," Mort insisted.

"You can't wear size 34 underwear," protested the exasperated tailor. "If you did, your eyes would bulge right out of their sockets!"

THE FIRST JEWISH PRESIDENT

It is the year 2012 and the first Jewish President of the United States has been elected. The first thing he does is to call his mother in Brooklyn.

He says, "Hello Ma! Guess what?"

She says, "What?"

He says, "I'm going to be the next President of the United States of America."

"That's nice," she says.

"Ma, you're coming to the Inauguration in January to see me being sworn in as the President of the United States."

"I can't come," she says.

"Why not?" he asks.

"I have nothing to wear," she says.

He says, "Ma, I'm going to be the President of the United States. I will send to your home the finest designers and tailors who will outfit you in perfect style."

"Okay," she says. "But I don't know where you live."

"Ma," he says, "I am the President of the United States. I will send Airforce One to New York to fly you to Washington. A limousine will pick you up at the airport and bring you to the White House."

"Okay," she says, "I'll come."

The day of the inauguration arrives. The new Jewish President is up on the stage being sworn in by the Chief Justice of the Supreme Court.

His mother is sitting in the first row next to the outgoing President. She nudges him in the side and says, "You see that man up there with the Chief Justice? His brother is a doctor."

DIARY ENTRIES OF A YOUNG WOMAN ON A CRUISE SHIP

MONDAY

Dear Diary,

What a wonderful cruise this is going to be! I felt singularly honored this evening. The Captain asked me to dine at his table.

TUESDAY

Dear Diary,

I spent the entire afternoon on the bridge with the Captain.

WEDNESDAY

Dear Diary,

The Captain made proposals to me unbecoming an officer and a gentleman.

THURSDAY

Dear Diary,

Tonight the Captain threatened to sink the ship if I do not give in to his indecent proposals!

FRIDAY

Dear Diary,

This afternoon I saved 1600 lives.

THE LOAN

A man who had recently been laid off from his job was sitting in his living room studying the bills that had accumulated over the past month. He spoke to his wife and told her that she would have to go to work in order to help with the expenses. She replied that she did not know of any job she could work at, since she had no experience in the business world.

He told her that she could she could go out in the street and do some tricks. She said that she did not know anything about prostitution. He said that did not matter; he would drive her downtown and park and if she wanted his help all she had to do was go back to the car and ask him what to do.

She put on a miniskirt and a tight sweater and he drove her downtown. She got out of the car and was walking along when a car drew up and the man in the car asked her if she would like to have some sex.

She said, "Wait a minute, I'll be right back."

She returned to the car and knocked on the window. Her husband said, "What's the problem?"

She said, "A man just stopped me and wants to have sex. What do I charge?"

He said, "Tell him $100."

She went back to the man's car and told him that he would have to pay $100. He said, "Oh damn, I only have $50."

She said, "Wait a minute, I'll be right back." She returned to her husband's car and knocked on the window. He rolled down the window and said, "Yes?"

She said, "He only has $50. What shall I do?"

He said "Tell him you can only give him a hand job for $50."

She went back to the man's car and told him that she could give him a hand job for the $50. He said, "Damn, that's not good," but agreed to take the hand job.

"Get in the car," he said. She sat down in the front seat next to him. He opened his pants and took out his huge appendage.

She gaped at his enormous tool and said, "Wait a minute, I'll be right back."

She returned to her husband's car and rapped on the window. He rolled down the window and said, "What is it this time?"

She said, "Can we lend him $50?"

MIRACLE

Doctor Bloom was known for miraculous cures for arthritis. He had a waiting room full of people when a little old lady, completely bent over in half, shuffled in slowly, leaning on her cane. When her turn came, she went into the doctor's office, and amazingly, emerged within half an hour walking completely erect with her head held high. A woman in the waiting room who had seen all this walked up to the little old lady and said, "It's a miracle! You walked in bent in half and now your walking erect. What did the doctor do?"

She answered, "Miracle, shmiracle...he gave me a longer cane."

COW FROM MINSK

In a little shtetl in Russia, there lived a small community of Jews who jointly owned a wonderful cow who gave milk, cream, and butter for the whole town. One day the cow developed a virus, got sick, and died. The villagers had a meeting and decided to purchase another cow to fill their needs. They decided that they would send to Moscow for a replacement. A man stood and up and said, "I have heard of a cow in Minsk that gives twice the amount of milk and butter that the average cow gives, and if this group agrees, I will go to Minsk and purchase the cow for the community." They all agreed, and the cow was acquired for the shtetl. The cow lived up to its reputation and all of the shtetl was happy with the results.

They had another meeting to talk about the good purchase that they had made. One man said, "Why don't we protect ourselves for the future. We will buy a bull, mate him with the cow and produce a calf." The villagers thought that was a good idea. The villagers bought a bull and brought him back to the community where he was put in the pasture with the cow.

The bull became interested in the cow and approached her from the right side. The cow moved to the left side. The bull decided to go to the left side and the cow moved to the right. Well, this went on all afternoon and the villagers were beside themselves. "How are we going get a calf if this continues to happen?" they said.

One man said, "Why don't we go and ask the rabbi? He is a very knowledgeable man and perhaps he can solve this problem." The villagers all agreed and went to the Shul to meet with the rabbi.

The rabbi welcomed into his study and said, "What can I do for you?" One of the men told the rabbi the story of how when the bull goes to the right, the cow goes to the left and when the bull goes to the left, the cow goes to the right. The rabbi reflected on this for a moment and then said "You bought this cow from Minsk. Right?"

Another man said, "Rabbi you are brilliant...such a learned man. How did you know that we bought this cow in Minsk?"

"Well," said the rabbi, "I married a woman from Minsk."

STRUDEL

Sam Cohen is 95 years old and is lying in bed, very, very sick. The doctor says that he will probably not last through the day. His children and wife have gathered at his house to see him off. While he is lying in bed sick and dying he can smell the special strudel that Mama is making in the kitchen. His daughter Selma comes into the room and says, "Oh Papa, I am so sorry for you. Is there anything I can do to make you more comfortable?"

Sam answers, "Selma, if I could just have a plate of Mama's special strudel, I would die a happy man."

Selma says, "Papa I'll go speak to Mama." Five minutes later Selma comes back and says, "Papa I am so sorry, Mama says the strudel is for after the funeral."

DONALD DUCK AND MINNIE MOUSE

Donald Duck and Minnie Mouse were up in a hotel room and decided that they wanted to have sex. The first thing Minnie asks is, "Do you have a condom?"

Donald says, "No."

Minnie tells Donald that if he doesn't get a condom that they can't have sex and suggests to Donald that he go buy a condom. She says that maybe they sell them at the front desk.

Donald proceeds downstairs and goes to the front desk. He asks the hotel clerk if they sell condoms. The clerk says, "Yes, we do," and pulls one out from under the desk and gives it to Donald. The clerk asks, "Would you like me to put that on your bill?"

Donald says, "NO! WHAT DO YOU THINK I AM? SOME KIND OF PERVERT?"

WAILING WALL

Aaron Cohen went to live in Israel in 1978. For 18 years, Aaron prayed at the Wailing Wall everyday, 6 hours a day. He did not miss one single day for 18 years. The editor of the Jerusalem Post heard about this and thought that it would make a good story. He sent a reporter to find Mr. Cohen at the Wall and interview him. The reporter found Mr. Cohen at the Wall and asked if he could interview him. Aaron said, "Why not? Go right ahead."

"Mr. Cohen," said the reporter, "Is it true that you have been praying at this Wall 6 hours a day for 18 years without missing a single day?"

"That's right, that's right," said Aaron.

"Tell me Mr. Cohen, what do you pray for?"

"Oh!" said Aaron. "I pray that my family will be healthy—that my children will go to college and become professionals."

"Do you pray for anything else, Mr. Cohen?"

"Yes, I pray that there will be world peace. That nations will get along with each other and there will be no nuclear holocaust."

"And is that everything you pray for?"

"No, I also pray that Israel and the Arab world will make peace and there will be no more terrorism."

"Mr. Cohen," said the reporter, "In the 18 years that you have been praying at the Wall, 6 hours a day, every day, have any of your prayers ever been answered?"

"NAW," said Aaron, "IT'S LIKE TALKING TO A WALL."

ICE FISHING

A drunk decides to go ice fishing. He gathers his gear and goes walking around until he finds a big patch of ice. He heads into the center of the ice and begins to saw a hole in the ice. All of a sudden, a loud booming voice comes out of the sky. "You will find no fish under that ice."

The drunk looks around, but sees no one. He starts sawing again. Once more, the voice speaks, "As I said before, there are no fish under the ice."

The drunk looks all around, high and low, but can't see a single soul. He picks up the saw and tries one more time to finish. Before he can even start cutting the huge voice interrupts. "I have warned you three times now. There are no fish!"

The drunk is now flustered and somewhat scared, so he asks the voice. "How do you know there are no fish? Are you God trying to warn me?"

"No," the voice replied.

"Who are you then?" asked the drunk.

"I am the manager of this hockey rink."

THE CAR

A Texan was traveling in Israel one very hot day. Developing a thirst for water, he stopped at a small house by the side of the road. He went up to the house and knocked on the door. A little old man opened the door and said, "Vell?"

The Texan said, "Sir, I am traveling in Israel on this very hot day and am extremely thirsty. I wonder if you could spare a glass of water?"

"Soitenly," said the little old man. "Come right in, make yourself at home and I will get you a nice cold glass of water."

"Thank you," said the Texan, as he downed the glass of water in two gulps. "Nice place you have here," he added. "How many rooms do you have?"

"Four rooms," said the little old man.

"At my big ranch in Texas, I have 24 rooms and a stable for 37 horses. Do you have any animals around the place?" asked the Texan.

"Oh sure," said the little old man. "I have four chickens and a goat in the backyard."

"At my big ranch in Texas, I have 2000 head of cattle and 135 horses," said the Texan. "How much land do you have around this place?"

"Oh," said the little old man, "I have 10 feet on the left side, 5 feet on the right side, and the backyard goes all the way back to 30 feet."

"Now let me tell you how much land I have at my BIG ranch in Texas," said the Texan. "In the morning, when I come out of my front door, and get in my BIG Cadillac, and drive, it takes me 9 hours to get to the end of my property."

"You know," said the little old man, "I HAD A CAR LIKE THAT ONCE."

GRAPES

A duck walks into a barroom. He asks the bartender, "Do you have any grapes?"

"No but the grocery store two blocks down the street sells grapes," the bartender replied.

The next day, the same duck walks into the same barroom and asks, "Do you have any grapes?"

"No, I told you yesterday that we don't have any grapes," said the bartender. "This a barroom not a grocery store. Now get out of here and don't come back."

The next day, the same duck walks into the same barroom and asks, "Do you have any grapes?"

The bartender looks at him. "No, we don't sell grapes here. This is a barroom not a grocery store. This is the third time that I've told you this. If you come back in here tomorrow and ask me for grapes, I'm going to nail your little web feet to the floor. NOW GET OUT OF HERE AND DON'T COME BACK."

The next day the same duck walks into the same barroom goes up to the bartender and asks, "Do you have any nails?"

"No," replies the bartender.

"Do you have any grapes?" says the duck.

ELEMENTARY MY DEAR WATSON

Sherlock Holmes and Dr. Watson went on a camping trip. As they lay down for the night, Holmes said, "Watson, look up into the sky and tell me what you see."

Watson said, "I see millions and millions of stars."

"And what does that tell you?"

"Astronomically," Watson replied, "It tells me that there are millions of galaxies and potentially billions of planets. Theologically, it tells me that God is great and that we are small and insignificant. Meteorologically, it tells me that we will have a beautiful day tomorrow. What does it tell you?"

"Somebody stole our tent."

THE INTERVIEW

A very devout nun dies and goes to heaven. Upon arrival she is greeted with ceremony and honor and told she may immediately have any wish she chooses while her place is prepared for her. She humbly and politely replies that she would like an audience with Holy Mary, if this is possible. Peter agrees on the spot and escorts her personally to a little door, hitherto unnoticed in the great vault of the firmament. He knocks softly.

There's a murmured reply from within and he opens the door and indicates to his guest to enter. Sitting in a plain chair is a middle-aged Jewish woman in the garb of the first century, knitting. The nun sits reverently for some time at Mary's feet and finally gestures so as to ask a question. Mary looks up from her knitting and indicates it's okay to ask.

"Reverend Mother, please tell me, you were chosen from all women to be the mother of God, you a simple Jewish woman I know, but if you could, can you just give me an inkling of what it felt like when it happened, when Jesus was born?"

With a distant look in her eyes she replies, "We were hoping for a girl."

THREE-LEGGED CHICKEN

A man is driving along a country road at about 40 mph. He looks out his passenger side window and sees a chicken running alongside his car. He says to himself, "How can a chicken run 40 mph?"

He looks carefully at the chicken and notices that the chicken has three legs. "Okay," he says "I'll show that chicken a thing or two."

He steps on the gas pedal and goes 50 mph. The chicken speeds up to 50 mph. "Oh, so you want to race," he says and speeds up to 60 mph. The chicken then zooms ahead over the horizon leaving the motorist in the dust.

Five minutes later the man notices a farmer standing by the side of the road. He stops his car and walks over to the farmer and says, "Did you see a three legged chicken run by here?"

The farmer replies, "Yeah, about 5 minutes ago, one went barreling by me."

The man says, "Where do those chickens come from?"

"Oh," says the farmer, "I raise them."

"Why do you do that?" asks the man.

"Well," says the farmer, "you see it's this way. I love drumsticks. My wife likes drumsticks and what if you have guest over for dinner and they like drumsticks?"

"I see," says the man. "That's a great idea. What do they taste like?"

"I dunno," says the farmer. "We've never been able to catch one."

ADAM'S RIB

Adam was walking around the Garden of Eden feeling very lonely. So God asked him, "What is wrong with you?"

Adam said he didn't have anyone to talk to. God said he was going to give him a companion and it would be a woman. God said, "This person will cook for you and wash your clothes. She will always agree with every decision you make. She will bear you children and never ask you to get up in the middle of the night to take care of them. She will not nag you, and will always be the first to admit she was wrong when you've had a disagreement. She will never have a headache, and will freely give you love and compassion whenever needed."

Adam asked God, "What will a woman like this cost?"

God replied, "An arm and a leg."

Adam said, "What can I get for a just a rib?"

The rest is history.

NAVAL OPERATIONS

This is the actual radio transmission with Canadian authorities off the coast of Newfoundland in October 1995. It was released by the Chief of Naval Operations on October 10th of that year.

CANADIANS: Please divert your course 15 degrees to the south to avoid collision.

AMERICANS: Recommend you divert your course 15 degrees to the north to avoid a collision.

CANADIANS: Negative. You will have to divert your course 15 degrees to the south to avoid a collision.

AMERICANS: This is the captain of a US Navy ship. I say again, divert YOUR course.

CANADIANS: No, I say again, you divert YOUR course.

AMERICANS: This is the Aircraft Carrier US LINCOLN, the second largest ship in the United States Atlantic Fleet. We are accompanied with three Destroyers, three Cruisers and numerous support vessels. I DEMAND that you change your course 15 degrees north. I say again, that's one-five degrees north, or counter-measures will be undertaken to ensure the safety of this ship.

CANADIANS: This is a lighthouse. Your call.

SINGLE LIFE

It is 7:30 am and a beautiful Florida morning at the Grand Hotel Condominium complex in Boca Raton. Ethel Goldstein, a widow of many years, goes down to the pool for her usual morning swim. At the pool, the only other person there is an attractive man that she has never seen before. Going over to introduce herself, Ethel says to him, "Excuse me sir, I don't believe I've ever seen you here before. Are you a member of the Condo Association?"

"I certainly am," he replies. "I have been away for a few years and just returned yesterday."

"Oh," she says, "Where have you been?"

He says, "I've been in jail."

Ethel says, "Why were you sent to jail?"

"Well," he says, "I murdered my wife and chopped her into 27 pieces with an axe."

"Oh," she says, "Then you're single, huh?"

WORDS OF WISDOM

A clean desk is a sign of a cluttered desk drawer.

Beat the five o'clock rush—leave work at noon.

Everyone has a photographic memory. Some just don't have any film.

Boycott shampoo! Demand the REAL poo!

What happens if you get scared half to death twice?

I used to have an open mind but my brains kept falling out.

How do you tell when you run out of invisible ink?

I used to be indecisive. Now I'm not sure.

I'm writing a book. I've got the page numbers done.

Wear short sleeves! Support your right to bare arms!

If at first you don't succeed, then skydiving is not for you.

I almost had a psychic girlfriend but she left me before we met.

Okay, so what's the speed of dark?

If we're not supposed to eat animals, why are they made of meat?

I couldn't repair your brakes, so I made your horn louder.

Experience is something you don't get until just after you need it.

All those who believe in telekinesis, raise my hand.

Depression is merely anger without enthusiasm.

When everything is coming your way, you're in the wrong lane.

Hard work pays off in the future. Laziness pays off now.

Shin: a device for finding furniture in the dark.

Many people quit looking for work when they find a job.

I intend to live forever. So far, so good.

Eagles may soar, but weasels don't get sucked into jet engines.

There are 24 hours in a day, and 24 beers in a case. You tell me: is it a coincidence?

When I'm not in my right mind, my left mind gets pretty crowded.

If at first you don't succeed, destroy all evidence that you tried.

For every action, there is an equal and opposite criticism.

No one is listening until you make a mistake.

Success always occurs in private, and failure in full view.

The colder the X-ray table, the more of your body is required to be on it.

The hardness of the butter is proportional to the softness of the bread.

The severity of the itch is proportional to the reach.

To steal ideas from one person is plagiarism; to steal from many is research.

The problem with the gene pool is that there is no lifeguard.

Monday is an awful way to spend one-seventh of your life.

The sooner you fall behind, the more time you'll have to catch up.

A clear conscience is usually the sign of a bad memory.

If you must choose between two evils, pick the one you've never tried before.

A fool and his money are soon partying.

Plan to be spontaneous tomorrow.

If you think nobody cares about you, try missing a couple of payments.

Drugs may lead to nowhere, but at least it's the scenic route.

I'd kill for a Nobel Peace Prize.

Bills travel through the mail at twice the speed of checks.

Borrow money from pessimists. They don't expect it back.

Half the people you know are below average.

Ninety-nine percent of lawyers give the rest a bad name.

According to a recent study, 42.7 percent of all statistics are made up on the spot.

CIRCLES, SQUARES, AND TRIANGLES

A young man, having trouble adjusting to life, decides to make an appointment with a psychiatrist. He arrives at the doctor's office and the doctor asks him to sit at a table with her. She produces a piece of paper and a pencil. She says, "I am going to draw some images and I want you to tell me your impression of them." She draws a circle on the paper and asks the patient, "What does that make you think of?"

"Sex," replies the young man.

"Alright, then what does this remind you of?" says the doctor as she draws a square on the piece of paper.

"That also reminds me of sex," says the young man.

"Very well," says the doctor. "What does this remind you of?" as she draws a triangle on the piece of paper.

"That definitely reminds me of sex," says the young man.

"You seem to be obsessed with sex," says the doctor.

The young man says, "I'm obsessed with sex? You're the one who is drawing the dirty pictures!"

THE MEMORIAL

One Rosh Hashanah morning, the rabbi noticed little Alex was staring up at the large plaque that hung in the foyer of the synagogue. It was covered with names, and small American flags were mounted on either side of it. The seven year old had been staring at the plaque for some time, so the rabbi walked up, stood beside the boy, and said quietly, "Good morning, Alex."

"Good morning Rabbi," replied the young man, still focused on the plaque. "Rabbi Bernstein, what is this?" Alex asked, pointing to the plaque.

"It's a memorial to all the young men and women who died in the service."

Soberly, they stood together, staring at the large plaque. Little Alex's voice was barely audible when he asked, "Which one, the Friday night service or the Saturday morning service?"

RECIPE FOR BEST EVER CHOCOLATE RUM CAKE

2 quarts rum

1 Tablespoon soda

1 cup butter

1/2 cup cocoa

4 large eggs

3 teaspoons lemon juice

1 teaspoon baking powder

1 teaspoon brown sugar

1 Tablespoon sugar and nuts

1 cup dried fruit

Before you start, sample the rum for quality.

Now go ahead and select a large mixing bowl. Check the rum again. It must be just right. To be sure of this, pour 1 cup of rum into a glass and drink it. Repeat.

With electric mixer, beat 1 cup of buerrer in the large flufffy bowl. Add 1 seaspoon of thugar and beat again. Drink another cup of rum to ensure quality.

Add 2 arge leggs, 2 cups fried druit and beat until high. If druit gets stuck in the beaters, pry it loose with a drewscriver. Sample the rum again.

Sift 3 cups of pepper or salt (it doesn't matter). Sample the rum again.

Sift 1/2 pint of lemon juice. Fold in chopped butter and strained nuts. Add 1 babblespoon of brown thugar or whatever color you find. Wix mel.

Grease oven and turn cake pan to 350 gredees. Now pour the whole mess in the boven and cake.

SUPERMARKET CLERK

A young gentleman was on his first day as a new clerk in a supermarket. A customer asked him if she could buy half a grapefruit. Not knowing what to do, he excused himself to ask the manager. "Some nut out there wants to buy half a grapefruit..." he began, and when he suddenly noticed that the customer had entered the office behind him, he continued, "...and this lovely lady would like to buy the other half."

The manager was impressed with the way the young clerk amicably resolved the problem and they later started chatting. "Where are you from?" asked the store manager.

"Lancaster, Pennsylvania," replied the clerk, "home of ugly women and great hockey teams."

"Oh, my WIFE is from Lancaster," challenged the manager.

Without skipping a beat, the clerk asked, "What team was she on?"

DOLLARS FOR ISRAEL

A little old Jewish man is going through customs at Lod airport in Jerusalem. He is carrying two very heavy black suitcases. The inspector asks him to please put the suitcases on the table and to open one of them. The suitcase is opened and the inspector sees that it is filled with one dollar bills. He says, "What are you doing with all these one dollar bills?"

The little old man says, "I was doing work for the UJA and I collected all these dollars for Israel. I would go into a men's room with my knife and wait for someone to start using a urinal. Then I told him to donate a dollar to Israel or I would cut it off."

The inspector said, "Very interesting. So what do you have in the other suitcase?"

"Well," said the little old man, "not everybody gave."

FRIENDLY WITCH

A creature rose up out of the surf and came ashore. Its garments were made of green sea lettuce. "I am the friendly Witch of the Sand," she said, "I am only going to sunbathe." The sun was terribly hot. Her skin began to bake and it turned as red as a ripe tomato! Have you ever seen...a baking lettuce and tomato Sand Witch?

THE WATCH

It is a bright sunny day in the park. A man is sitting on one of the benches reading the New York Times. Along comes another man in a long black raincoat and a matching hat. He is moving very slowly as he seems to be carrying two large and heavy suitcases.

Breathing deeply, he approaches the bench where the first man is reading. When he reaches the bench, with an exhausted sigh he drops the suitcases on the ground. Just then his watch rings and announces: "It is now ten minutes past two. The wind is from the west at 10 miles per hour and it looks like we will have a pleasant day."

The man on the bench stops reading and says, "What a great watch. Where can I get a watch like that?"

The man with suitcase says, "If you like I could sell this one to you for $50.00."

"Wow," says the man with the New York Times. "I'll take it." The trade is made and the man gets up from bench and walks away.

"Stop! Wait!" shouts the man with the long black coat.

"Why?" asks the man with his new watch.

"YOU FORGOT THE BATTERIES!"

VOW OF SILENCE

A guy joins a monastery and takes a vow of silence: he's allowed to say two words every seven years. After the first seven years, the elders bring him in and ask him for his two words.

"Cold floors," he says.

They nod and send him away. Seven years pass. They bring him in for his two words.

He clears his throat and says, "Bad food."

They nod and send him away. Seven more years pass. Once again they bring him in for his two words.

"I quit," he says.

"That's not surprising," the elders say, "You've done nothing but complain since you got here."

JOE'S BARBER SHOP

A man walked in to Joe's Barber Shop for his regular haircut. As he snips away, Joe asks, "What's up?" The man proceeds to explain he's taking a vacation to Rome.

"ROME?!" Joe says. "Why would you want to go there? It's a crowded dirty city full of Italians! You're crazy to go to Rome! So how ya getting there?"

"We're taking TWA," the man replies.

"TWA?!" yells Joe. "They're a terrible airline. Their planes are old, their flight attendants are ugly and they're always late! So where you staying in Rome?"

The man says, "We'll be at the downtown International Marriott."

"That DUMP?!" says Joe. "That's the worst hotel in the city! The rooms are small, the service is surly and slow and they're overpriced! So whatcha doing when you get there?"

The man says, "We're going to go see the Vatican and hope to see the Pope."

"HA! That's rich!" laughs Joe. "You and a million other people trying to see him. He'll look the size of an ant. Boy, good luck on THIS trip. You're going to need it!"

A month later, the man comes in for his regular haircut. Joe says, "Well, how did that trip to Rome turn out? Betcha TWA gave you the worst flight of your life!"

"No, quite the opposite," explained the man. "Not only were we on time in one of their brand new planes, but it was full and they bumped us up to first class. The food and wine were wonderful, and I had a beautiful 28 year old flight attendant who waited on me hand and foot!"

"Hmmm," Joe says, "Well, I bet the hotel was just like I described."

"No, quite the opposite! They'd just finished a $25 million remodeling. It's the finest hotel in Rome, now. They were overbooked, so they apologized and gave us the Presidential suite for no extra charge!"

"Well," Joe mumbles, "I KNOW you didn't get to see the Pope!"

"Actually, we were quite lucky. As we toured the Vatican, a Swiss guard tapped me on the shoulder and explained the Pope likes to personally meet some of the visitors, and if I'd be so kind as to step into this private room and wait, the Pope would personally greet me. Sure enough, 5 minutes later, the Pope walked through the door and shook my hand. I knelt down as he spoke a few words to me."

Impressed, Joe asks, "Tell me, please! What'd he say?"

"Oh, not much really. Just, 'Where'd you get that awful haircut?'"

PROFESSIONAL RIVALRY

Two attorneys boarded a flight out of Seattle. One sat in the window seat while the other sat in the middle seat. Just before takeoff, a physician boarded the plane and took the aisle seat next to the two attorneys. The physician kicked off his shoes, wiggled his toes and was settling in when the attorney in the window seat said, "I think I'll get up and get a Coke."

"No problem," said the physician, "I'll get it for you." While he was gone, one of the attorneys picked up the physician's shoe and spat in it.

When he returned with the Coke, the other attorney said, "That looks good, I think I'll have one too."

Again, the physician obligingly went to fetch it and while he was gone, the other attorney picked up the other shoe and spat in it.

The physician returned and they all sat back and enjoyed the flight. As the plane was landing, the physician slipped his feet into his shoes and knew immediately what had happened. "How long must this go on?" he asked. "This fighting between our professions? This hatred? This animosity? This spitting in shoes and pissing in Cokes?"

GOLF

The other day I came home from work and was greeted by my wife dressed in a very sexy nightie and holding a couple of short velvet ropes. "Tie me up," she purred, "and you can do anything you want."

So, I tied her up and went golfing.

THE GUEST

Seymour was invited by his friend Larry to play golf with him at his country club. It was very nice day out on the links so they decided to play 18 holes. After the game was over they went over to the clubhouse. Larry said that he had to make an important phone call and suggested that Seymour go take a shower.

When Seymour was leaving the shower he heard female voices and realized that he had mistakenly showered in the women's locker room. He put a towel over his head and ran out of the locker room. Three women golfers were coming in at the same time that he was leaving.

The first woman said, "He's not my husband!"

The second woman said, "He's certainly not my husband!"

The third woman chimes in, "Hell, he's not even a member of this club!"

FOOD FOR THOUGHT

A doctor was addressing a large audience in Tampa. "The material we put into our stomachs is enough to have killed most of us sitting here, years ago. Red meat is awful. Soft drinks corrode your stomach lining. Chinese food is loaded with MSG. High fat diets can be disastrous, and none of us realizes the long-term harm caused by the germs in our drinking water." He paused. "But there is one thing that is the most dangerous of all, and we all have, or will eat it. Would anyone care to guess what food causes the most grief and suffering for years after eating it?"

After several seconds of quiet, a small 85 year old Jewish man sitting in the front row, raised his hand and said, "Vedding cake?"

FATHER

St. Peter got fed up with standing at the Pearly gates and giving or denying access to heaven, so Jesus offered to take over. After a short while, a man came up to him. "I'm looking for my son," he said.

"And who are you?" asked Jesus.

"I suppose I'm the closest thing he has to a father," said the man.

"What do you do?" asked Jesus curiously.

"I suppose you could say I'm a carpenter," said the man.

"And does your son have holes in his hands and feet?" asked Jesus excitedly.

"He does!" shouted the man.

"Father!" cried Jesus.

"Pinocchio!" shouted Geppetto.

HORSE RACING

A man was sitting quietly reading his paper one morning, peacefully enjoying himself, when his wife sneaked up behind him and clobbered him on the back of his head with a huge cast-iron frying pan.

"What was that for?" the man screamed in pain.

"What is that piece of paper in your pants pocket with the name Marylou written on it?" his wife demanded.

"Oh, honey. Don't you remember 2 weeks ago when I went to the horse races? Marylou was the name of one of the horses I bet on."

The wife seemed satisfied and headed off to do some work around the house, feeling a bit sheepish. Three days later the man was once again sitting in his chair when his wife sneaked up and again hit him on the head with a cast-iron frying pan.

"What's that for this time?" the man shouted, clutching his head.

"Your horse called."

THE SPOON

Last week I took some friends out to a new restaurant, and noticed that the waiter who took our order carried a spoon in his shirt pocket. It seemed a little strange, but I ignored it. However, when the busboy brought out water and utensils, I noticed he also had a spoon in his shirt pocket, then looked around the room and saw that all the staff had spoons in their pockets.

When the waiter come back to serve our soup, I asked, "Why the spoon?"

"Well," he explained, "the restaurant's owners hired Anderson Consulting, experts in efficiency, to revamp all our processes. After several months of statistical analysis, they concluded that customers drop their spoons 73.84 percent more often than any other utensil. This represents a drop frequency of approximately three spoons per table per hour. If our personnel is prepared to deal with that contingency, we can reduce the number of trips back to the kitchen and save 1.5 man-hours per shift."

As luck would have it, I dropped my spoon and he was able to replace it with his spare spoon. He said, "I'll get another spoon next time I go to the kitchen instead of making an extra trip to get it right now."

I was rather impressed. The waiter served our main course and I continued to look around. I then noticed that there was a very thin string hanging out of the waiter's fly. Looking around, I noticed that all the waiters had the same string hanging from their flies.

My curiosity got the better of me and before he walked off, I asked the waiter, "Excuse me, but can you tell me why you have that string right there?"

"Oh, certainly!" he answered, lowering his voice. "Not everyone is as observant as you. That consulting firm I mentioned also found out that we can save time in the restroom."

"How so?" I asked.

"See," he continued, "by tying this string to the tip of you-know-what, we can pull 'it' out over the urinal without touching it, and that way eliminate the need to wash our hands, shortening the time spent in the restroom by 76.39 percent."

"Okay, that makes sense, but if the string helps you get it out, how do you put it back in?"

"Well," he whispered, lowering his voice even further, "I don't know about the others, but I use the spoon."

RODNEY DANGERFIELD'S BEST ONE-LINERS

1. A girl phoned me the other day and said, "Come on over, there's nobody home." So I went over. Nobody was home.
2. If it weren't for pickpockets I'd have no sex life at all.
3. And we were poor too. Why if I wasn't born a boy... I'd have nothing to play with.
4. During sex, my girlfriend always wants to talk to me. Just the other night she called me from a hotel.
5. One day as I came home early from work, I saw a guy jogging naked. I said to the guy, "Hey buddy... what are you doing that for?" He said, "Because you came home early."
6. It's been a rough day. I got up this morning, put on a shirt, and a button fell off. I picked up my briefcase and the handle came off. I'm afraid to go to the bathroom.
7. When I played in the sandbox, the cat kept covering me.
8. I could tell that my parents hated me. My bath toys were a toaster and a plugged-in extension cord.
9. My mother never breastfed me. She told me that she only liked me as a friend.
10. When I was born, the doctor came out to the waiting room and said to my father, "I'm very sorry. We did everything we could, but he pulled through."
11. My mother had morning sickness after I was born.
12. I remember the time I was kidnapped and they sent a piece of my finger to my father. He said he wanted more proof.
13. Once when I was lost, I saw a policeman and asked him to help me find my parents. I said to him, "Do you think we'll ever find them?" He said, "I don't know, kid—there are so many places they can hide."
14. My wife made me join a bridge club. I jump off next Tuesday.
15. I worked in a pet shop and people kept asking how big I'd get.

16. I went to see my doctor. "Doctor, every morning when I get up and look in the mirror, I feel like throwing up. What's wrong with me?" He said, "I don't know but your eyesight is perfect."

17. My psychiatrist told me I'm going crazy. I told him, "If you don't mind I'd like a second opinion." He said, "All right, you're ugly too!"

A CHANCE ENCOUNTER

A man was eating in a fancy restaurant, and there was a gorgeous blonde eating at the next table. He had been checking her out all night, but lacked the nerve to go talk to her.

Suddenly she sneezed and her glass eye went flying out of its socket towards the man. With his quick reflexes, he caught it in mid-air.

"Oh my God, I am sooooo sorry," the woman said as she popped her eye back in the socket. "Let me buy you dinner to make it up to you."

They enjoyed a wonderful dinner together and afterwards the woman invited him back to her place for a drink. They went back to her house, and after a bit she brought him into the bedroom and began undressing him.

The couple had wild, passionate sex many times during the night. The next morning when he awoke, she had already gotten up and brought him breakfast in bed. The guy was amazed. "You know, you are the perfect woman. Are you this nice to every guy you meet?"

"No," she replied. "You just happened to catch my eye."

UNFAITHFUL WIFE

Morris returns from a long business trip and finds out that his wife has been unfaithful during his time away.

"Who was it?" he yells. "That alta Kakker Goldstein?"

"No," replied his wife. "It wasn't Goldstein."

"Was it Feldman, that dirty old man?"

"No, not him."

"Aha! Then it must have been that idiot Rabinovich!"

"No, it wasn't Rabinovich either."

Morris is now fuming. "What's the matter?" he cries. "None of my friends are good enough for you?!"

HOT DOGS

Two immigrants arrived in America. On their first day off the boat in New York City, they spied a hot dog vendor in the street.

"Do they eat dogs in America?" one asked the other.

"I dunno."

"Well, we're going to live here, so we might as well learn to do as they do." So they each bought a hot dog wrapped in wax paper and sat down to eat them on a nearby park bench.

One immigrant looked inside his wax paper, then over at the other and asked, "What part did you get?"

THE DONATION

"Hello, is this Rabbi Schwartz?"

"It is."

"This is the IRS. Can you help us?"

"I can."

"Do you know a Sam Cohen?"

"I do."

"Is he a member of your congregation?"

"He is."

"Did he donate $10,000 to your synagogue?"

"He will."

FRIENDS

A chicken and a horse were very good friends and spent most of their spare time together in a meadow. The horse chomped on the clumps of grass and the chicken pecked away at all the seeds.

One day the horse, not noticing where he was going, fell into a deep hole and couldn't get out. He yelled for the chicken and asked him to run to the farmhouse and bring the farmer back in order to pull him out of the hole.

The chicken ran as fast as he could to the farmhouse to look for the farmer. He looked everywhere for the farmer but could not find him.

The farmer's big Mercedes was parked alongside the house. The chicken looked inside and noticed that the keys were in the ignition. So the chicken got a length of strong rope, put it in the car and drove out to the meadow.

He fastened one end of the rope to the horse and the other end to the bumper. Then he stepped on the gas and pulled his friend out of the hole. His friend thanked him and they went back to their chomping and pecking.

A couple of days later, wouldn't you know it, the chicken fell into the same hole. He screamed for the horse to run to the house and get the farmer to come and save him.

The horse said, "Don't worry, this is something that I can handle myself."

He then straddled himself over the hole and said to the chicken: "Grab hold of my thingy and I will pull you out to safety."

The chicken grabbed the horse's thingy and sure enough the horse pulled the chicken out of the hole.

The moral of this story is: If you are hung like a horse, you don't need a big Mercedes to pick up a chick.

TWO PIECES OF STRING

Two pieces of string are walking down the street when they stop in front of a bar.

One piece of string says, "You know, I really need a drink."

The other piece of string says, "Well, you can't go into this bar. They don't serve string."

"Well, I really do need a drink. I'm going in and try anyway."

"Okay," says the other piece of string. "Don't say I didn't warn you."

So the first piece of string walks up to the bar and says he wants order a drink. The bartender looks at the piece of string and says, "Sorry, but we don't serve string at this bar."

The piece of string goes outside and tells his friend that they wouldn't serve him. "Didn't I tell you so?" asked his friend.

"But I really need to get a drink badly," says the first piece of string.

"Okay," says his friend. "Let's see what we can do."

He ties a knot in the first piece of string and then unravels part of one end. "Now," he says, "go in and see if the bartender recognizes you as a piece of string."

The first piece of string walks up to the bar. The bartender looks him, scratches his head, and says, "You remind me of a piece of string."

The first piece of string shakes his head no and says, "I'm a FRAYED KNOT."

TANDJEWBERRYMUD

For full effect, read this joke aloud.

The following is a telephone exchange between a hotel guest and room service at a hotel in Asia. It was recorded and published in the *Far East Economic Review*.

Room Service (RS): "Morny. Ruin sorbees."

Guest (G): "Sorry, I thought I dialed room-service."

RS: "Rye..Ruin sorbees. Morny! Djewish to odor sumteen??"

G: "Uh…yes…I'd like some bacon and eggs"

RS: "Ow July den?"

G: "What??"

RS: "Ow July den? Pry, boy, pooch?"

G : "Oh, the eggs! How do I like them? Sorry, scrambled please."

RS: "Ow July dee bayhcem? Crease?"

G: "Crisp will be fine."

RS : "Hokay. An san toes?"

G: "What?"

RS: "San toes. July san toes?"

G: "I don't think so."

RS: "No? Judo one toes??"

G: "I feel really bad about this, but I don't know what 'judo one toes' means."

RS: "Toes! toes! Why djew Don Juan toes? Ow bow inglish mopping we bother?"

G: "English muffin!! I've got it! You were saying 'Toast.' Fine. Yes, an English muffin will be fine."

RS: "We bother?"

G: "No…just put the bother on the side."

RS: "Wad?"

G: "I mean butter...just put it on the side."

RS: "Copy?"

G: "Sorry?"

RS: "Copy...tea...mill?"

G: "Yes. Coffee please, and that's all."

RS: "One Minnie. Ass strangle ache, crease baychem, tossys inglish mopping we bother honey sigh, and copy. Rye??"

G: "Whatever you say."

RS: "Tendjewberrymud!"

G : "You're welcome."

WIDOWHOOD AND REMARRIAGE

In a small town, the rabbi died. His widow, the Rebbetzin, was so disconsolate that the people of the town decided that she ought to get married again. But the town was so small that the only eligible bachelor was the town butcher.

The poor Rebbetzin was somewhat dismayed because she had been wed to a scholar, and the butcher had no great formal education. However, she did not want to stay lonely for the rest of her life, so she agreed, and they were married.

After the marriage she went to the mikvah (a Jewish ritual bath to get rid of impurities). Then she went home to prepare to light the candles.

The butcher leaned over to her and said, "My mother told me that after the mikvah and before lighting the candles, it's good to have sex." So they did.

Then she lit the candles. He leaned over again and said, "My father told me that after lighting the candles it's good to have sex." So they did.

They went to bed after saying their prayers. When they awoke he said to her, "My grandmother said that before you go to the synagogue it's good to have sex." So they did.

After praying all morning, they came home to rest, and again he whispers in her ear, "My grandfather says after praying it's good to have sex." So they did.

On Sunday she went out to shop for food and met an old friend who asked, "So how is the new husband and your marriage progressing?"

She replied, "Well, as you know, he is no scholar, but he certainly comes from a wonderful family."

NOTHING

It is the evening of Yom Kippur and the rabbi has worked himself into a state of religious fervor. He prostrates himself on the floor and cries: "Lord, Lord, you are so mighty and powerful. In your eyes I am nothing, nothing."

The cantor, also caught up in this religious fervor, prostrates himself on the floor next to the rabbi and says: "Lord, Mighty Lord, in your eyes I am nothing."

Irving Schwartz, sitting in the third row observing what is going on, is also carried away with religious fervor.

Irving moves out into the aisle and prostrates himself on the floor and cries out, "Lord, in your eyes I am nothing."

The rabbi, observing the antics of Irving, pokes the cantor in the ribs and says, "Look who thinks he's nothing."

ROOM 436

A man is in a hotel lobby. He wants to ask the clerk a question. As he turns to go to the front desk, he accidentally bumps into a woman beside him and as he does his elbow goes into her breast. They are both quite startled.

The man turns to her and says, "Ma'am, if your heart is as soft as your breast, I know you'll forgive me."

She replies, "If your dick is as hard as your elbow, I'm in room 436."

GOD

One day a guy named Irving was sitting in his living room trying to understand the nature of God. All of a sudden he hears a voice in the room saying, "Irving, this is God. Did you want to ask me a question?"

"Yes, God, I did," says Irving. "God, how long is a million years to you?"

God answers, "A million years is like a minute to me."

Then Irving asks, "How much is a million dollars to you?"

And God replies, "A million dollars is like a penny to me."

Then Irving says, "God, I'm a good man. I go to synagogue every Saturday and attend services on Yom Kippur. Do you think that you could give me a million dollars?"

And God says, "Wait a minute."

THE POPE

The Pope comes to America. Of course, he's very busy saying Masses and attending rallies, dinners, and events. For security, he has the same limousine driver every day.

One evening at a banquet, he sees a chance to sneak away unnoticed. He goes out back, finds his limo, and knocks on the window.

The driver is lounging in the rear seat eating a huge sandwich with his feet up on the seat. The driver says, "Your Holiness! I'm so sorry. Where can I take you? Forgive me!"

The Pope says, "Sit, eat, my son. Truthfully, I'd like to take the car for a drive. I'm the Pope, and everything is done for me. I've never driven an automobile. Please allow me."

The driver answers, "Certainly, your Holiness. Let me assist you."

The Pope insists, "Sit, my son. Finish your dinner."

The Pope gets into the car and begins to drive. Naturally, he is not very good at it, as he has never driven before. After hitting several parked cars, lampposts, and stop signs, he is pulled over by a state trooper.

The trooper gets out of his cruiser, approaches the driver's side window, and knocks. The Pope lowers the window. The trooper eyes the scene and retreats to his cruiser. Immediately he grabs his cell phone and calls the governor.

The trooper says, "Governor, this is state trooper Wilson. I've just pulled over the most important person in the world for a serious traffic violation but I don't know what to do."

The governor, very excited, says, "Who do you have there? The President? I will speak to the White House Chief of Staff. I'll straighten this out."

The trooper answers, "No, it's not the President. He's the most important person in the world!"

The governor says, "Well, who do you have? The United Nations Secretary General? I'll speak to the UN staff. Diplomatic immunity is a very sacred thing, you know."

The trooper says, "No, no. I've already told you. He's the most important person in the world, even more important than the President of the United States or the UN Secretary General!"

The governor, now frustrated, says, "Dammit, Wilson, who the hell did you pull over?"

And the trooper replies, "I have no idea, sir, but he's sitting in the back seat of a limo eating a sandwich, and the Pope is his driver!"

LIMERICKS

There was a young sailor from Brighton
Who remarked to his girl, "You're a tight one."
    She replied, "'Pon my soul,
        You're in the wrong hole:
There's plenty of room in the right one."

There was a young fellow named Goody
Who claimed that he wouldn't, but would he?
    If he found himself nude
        With a gal in the mood,
The question's not would he, but could he?

There was a young plumber of Leigh
Who was plumbing a girl by the sea.
    She said, "Stop your plumbing,
        There's somebody coming!"
Said the plumber, still plumbing, "It's me."

There was a young fellow named Skinner
Who took a young lady to dinner.
    At a quarter to nine
        They sat down to dine;
At twenty to ten, it was in her.
Skinner?
No, the dinner.

There was a young girl who begat
Three brats, by the name Nat, Pat, and Tat.
    It was fun in the breeding
    But hell in the feeding,
When she found there was no tit for Tat.

A notorious whore named Miss Hearst
In the weakness of men is well versed.
    Reads a sign o'er the head
    Of her well-rumpled bed:
"The customer always comes first."

A tutor who tooted the flute
Tried to tutor two tooters to toot.
    Said the two to the tutor,
    "Is it harder to toot, or
To tutor two tooters to toot?"

A flea and a fly in a flue
Were imprisoned, so what could they do?
    Said the fly, "Let us flee."
    Said the flea, "Let us fly."
So they flew through a flaw in the flue.

THE SHOPLIFTER

Mildred Brown, of Del Ray Beach in Florida, was caught shoplifting at the local supermarket. Malcolm Brown, her husband of many years, was very upset with this situation. He said to Mildred, "How could you do such a thing? You have brought disgrace upon your family. I will never forgive you for this."

On Monday they went down to the courthouse, where Mildred was expected to appear before the judge and receive sentence. When they arrived, the judge said, "Mildred, how could you do something like this?"

Mildred said, "Judge, I am so sorry, I will never do this again."

"Mildred," said the judge, "what did you take from the supermarket?"

Mildred answered, "I took a can of peaches."

"How many peaches were in the can?" asked the judge.

Mildred said, "Five peaches."

"Mildred," said the judge, "I am going to sentence you to one day in jail for each of the peaches."

Malcolm said, "Ask her about the can of peas."

THE THIRSTY ARAB

A very thirsty Arab wanders amid the dunes of the Sahara Desert and angrily ponders his parched plight. As he stumbles, he sees something far off in the distance.

Hoping to find water, he walks toward the image. As he approaches, the Arab comes upon an old Jew. The Jew is seated at a card table, with a selection of beautiful neckties, neatly displayed.

In a tone nearing rage, the Arab exclaims, "Please, I'm dying of thirst! Give me water!"

The Jew replies quietly, "I'm sorry, I don't have any water. Why don't you buy a nice tie? This one goes beautifully with your robes."

The Arab shouts vehemently, "Idiot! I don't want a tie, I want water!"

The Jew says, "Okay, so don't buy a tie. But to show you I am a nice guy, I am going to let you in on a little secret. If you walk over that hill there, and go about 4 miles, you will find a nice restaurant. They will give you all the water you desire."

Recalling his manners, the Arab politely thanks the Jew. The Arab then walks over the hill, and disappears.

Three hours later, the Arab crawls back to the Jew's card table. The old Jew is surprised to see the Arab at his table again and says, "I told you to walk about 4 miles over that hill. Couldn't you find the restaurant?"

The Arab rasped, "I found it all right, but they wouldn't let me in without a tie."

THE GENIE

To celebrate their seventh anniversary, a man and his wife spend the weekend at an exclusive golf resort. He is a pretty good golfer, but she only just started. When they head down to the golf course after a lavish lunch and a bottle of champagne, they notice a beautiful mansion a couple of hundred yards behind the first hole.

"Let's be extra careful, honey," the husband says, "If we damage that house over there, it'll cost us a fortune."

The wife nods, tees off and—bang!—sends the ball right through the window of the mansion.

"Jesus Christ," the husband says. "I told you to watch out for that house. Alright, let's go up there, apologize and see what the damage is."

They walk up to the house and knock on the door.

"Come on in," a voice in the house says.

The couple opens the door and enters the foyer. The living room is a mess. There are pieces of glass all over the floor and a broken bottle near the window. A man sits on the couch.

When the couple enters the room, he gets up and says, "Are you the guys who just broke my window?"

"Um, yeah," the husband replies. "Sorry about that."

"Not at all, it's me who has to thank you. I'm a genie and I was trapped in that bottle for a thousand years. You've just released me. To show my gratitude, I'm allowed to grant each of you a wish. But—I'll require one favor in return."

"Really? That's great!" the husband says. "I want a million dollars a year for the rest of my life."

"No problem—that's the least I can do. And you, what do you want?" the genie asks, looking at the wife.

"I want a house in every country of the world," the wife says.

The genie smiles. "Consider it done."

"And what's this favor we must grant in return, genie?" the husband asks.

"Well, since I've been trapped in that stupid bottle for the last one thousand years, I haven't had sex with a woman for a very long time. My wish is to sleep with your wife."

The husband scratches his head, looks at his wife and says, "Well, we did get a lot of money and all these houses, honey. So I guess I'm fine if it's alright with you."

The genie and the wife disappear in a bedroom upstairs and make love for three hours, while the husband stays in the living room.

When they are done, the genie rolls over, looks at the wife and asks, "How old exactly is your husband?"

"Thirty-one," she replies.

"And he still believes in genies? That's amazing!"

PIG

A man is driving up a steep, narrow mountain road.

A woman is driving down the same road. As they pass each other, the woman leans out the window and yells, "PIG!!"

The man immediately leans out his window and replies, "BITCH!!"

They each continue on their way, and as the man rounds the next curve, he crashes into a pig in the middle of the road.

A PARKING SPACE

A man was driving down the street in a lather because he has an important meeting and couldn't find a parking space.

Looking up to heaven, he said, "Lord, take pity on me. If you find me a parking space, I promise to go to church every Sunday for the rest of my life and give up swearing."

Miraculously, a spot opened right in front of the building.

The man looked up and said, "Never mind. I found one."

ARRANGED MARRIAGE

A good Hasidic family is most concerned that their 30-year-old son is unmarried. So, they call a marriage broker and ask him to find their son a good wife. The broker comes over to their house and spends a long time asking questions of the son and his parents as to what they want in a wife/daughter-in-law. They give a long shopping list of requirements.

The marriage broker takes a long time looking, and finally asks to visit the family again. He then tells them of a wonderful woman he has found.

He says she's just the right age for the son...She keeps a Kosher home, she regularly attends synagogue and knows the prayers by heart...she is a wonderful cook...she loves children and wants a large family. And, to crown it all off, she's gorgeous.

After hearing all this, the family is very impressed and begins to get excited about the prospects of a wedding in the near future.

But the son pauses and asks inappropriately, "Is she also good in bed?"

The marriage broker answers, "Some say yes...some say no."

ABOUT THE AUTHOR

Bob Hoffman started collecting jokes more than 25 years ago when his good friend Wilbur Talisman began telling him fantastic jokes. **The Very Best Jokes of The Century** contains close to 100 of the best jokes in Bob's collection. Bob continues to collect jokes and would appreciate receiving good jokes from new sources.

Bob lives with his long-suffering wife Evie of 57 years who has had to listen to all of his jokes for 25 years. He enjoys having fun with his daughter Laura; three sons: Mark, David, and Jon; granddaughter Becky and grandson Josh.

Bob imagines himself a standup comedian and at the drop of a hat will corner an unsuspecting victim and proceed to try out a joke on him. Bob inherits his sense of humor from his father who once said to him, "I'll get even with you when you have children." Bob never really understood the meaning of his father's saying since he has not had one hour of aggravation or worry from his four wonderful children in over 50 years of family life.

Bob hopes that everyone will enjoy reading these jokes as much as he has enjoyed telling them. Enough said: onto fun, frivolity, and hysterical laughter.

Bob Hoffman

E-Mail Bob at: hoffy17@comcast.net